AF824214

CHARGED WITH A CRIME IN WESTERN PA?

Valuable information from a Pittsburgh Criminal Defense Attorney and a Nationwide Top 100 Criminal Defense Lawyer

FRANK C. WALKER, II

WWW.FRANKWALKERLAW.COM

Client Testimonials

"I would like to thank Mr. Walker and his firm for all the hard work they have done to settle this delicate matter for me and continue to strive to get the rest of the case expunged in a timely manner. I appreciate the time and consideration throughout this difficult process. Frank made me feel very comfortable throughout the last few months and I will thank him years to come. Thank you again!" – **Pittsburgh Client**

....

"Frank Walker is a skilled attorney, who can relate to the real legal needs of his clients. Whenever I sought his legal help, attorney Walker was quick to respond with a listening ear. Whenever I had trouble finding a good defense attorney in Pittsburgh - Frank Walker was there for me. I recommend his law firm to anyone who is in need of a personable and reputable attorney. I speak so highly of attorney Walker that my sister thought he was paying me for the compliments! If you ever need a skilled attorney - call Frank Walker (trust me, I know)!" - **Pittsburgh Client**

....

"Frank Walker Law is a great defense attorney. No matter what you have been charged with, Frank Walker will work for you to ensure you get the best outcome possible. He helped me in a very difficult situation, I'm sure he'll do the same for you." - **Pittsburgh Client**

Disclaimer

This publication is intended for informational purposes only. The material contained herein does not constitute legal advice, nor does reading this material create an attorney-client relationship with Attorney Walker or Frank Walker Law.

If you are facing legal issues, whether criminal or civil, seek professional legal counsel to get your questions answered.

Frank Walker Law
3000 Lewis Run Road
Clairton, Pennsylvania 15025
(412) 532-6805
www.FrankWalkerLaw.com

Charged With a Crime in Western PA?
by Frank C. Walker, II
Copyright ©2018 Frank C. Walker, II

All rights reserved. This book is protected under the copyright laws of the United States of America. This book may not be copied or reprinted for commercial gain or profit.

ISBN 978-1-63360-088-1

For Worldwide Distribution
Printed in the U.S.A.

Introducing Attorney Frank Walker

My name is Frank C. Walker, II and I am the owner of Frank Walker Law. I have been practicing criminal defense law since 2005 and have offices conveniently located in Pittsburgh, Pennsylvania, and Morgantown, West Virginia. I am licensed to practice law in all state and federal courts of Pennsylvania and West Virginia, including the United States Supreme Court.

For as long as I can remember, the notion of helping people drove my desire to be a criminal defense attorney. I wanted to help people who find themselves in difficult circumstances resolve their problems and be able to speak on their behalf. It is an awesome responsibility to heed the call of someone who comes to me and says, "I'm in trouble . . . I need your help . . . and I'm trusting you to help me with my case and my freedom." Criminal defense work is unique in that, at the heart of it, it is just my client and I fighting the state or federal government.

I started my legal career with the Allegheny County Office of Conflict Counsel when that office first opened in 2005. The office was created as the parallel office to the Allegheny County Office of the Public Defender for the purpose of representing defendants who had a conflict of interest with the Public Defender's Office for any number of reasons. For example, imagine there are two people in a car when the car is stopped by police, who find a gun in the car. Both passengers claim that the gun belongs to the other person. Neither person can afford to hire an attorney, so they go to the Office of the Public Defender. The defender is not able to represent both parties due to the inherent conflict of interest. Therefore, the public defender would keep one defendant, and send the other person to the Office of the Conflict Counsel.

In the beginning, the comparison between the two offices was stark: The Public Defender's office had about 40 attorneys and support staff, while the Office of Conflict Counsel had a staff of four. We accepted the challenge and handled all criminal hearings, jury trials, appeals, and Post-Conviction Relief Act petitions. My time spent with that office was a whirlwind experience that formed the foundation for my career.

From the Office of Conflict Counsel, I went to a medium-sized Pittsburgh law firm to work in the Criminal Defense and Civil Litigation Department. After countless criminal and civil jury trials, hearings, and other legal proceedings, I finally fulfilled my lifelong dream of starting my own law practice in 2011 when I started Frank Walker Law. Now, as an owner of my own law practice, I can select my cases, focus on specific areas of criminal defense law, and practice in many areas of the state and region.

Book Overview

This book is in a question-and-answer format with the interviewer asking Attorney Walker common questions from the client's point of view. The goal of the book is to offer an overview to the criminal justice system so you will know what to expect if you are arrested, cited, or under investigation for a criminal offense.

How Do you Know When You are the Subject of a Criminal Investigation?

Interviewer: Let's get into it: How do people know they are under criminal investigation?

Frank Walker: Sometimes it is obvious. Let's say you leave a bar and you get into a fight, and the police show up. If you are being questioned, in handcuffs, in the back of a cop car, and headed to the police station to get fingerprinted, it is safe to say that you know you are under investigation, and that you are under arrest. That is probably the most obvious scenario.

You may not be aware that you are under criminal investigation.

The not-so-obvious scenario is when your friends are calling you to let you know that police officers have been calling them and asking questions about you. Or detectives have requested that you to come down to the police station to answer some questions. You may think, "I'll just go down to the police station and clear this up."

The next thing you know, you are handcuffed and getting a free ride to the local jail, all because you just talked your way into an arrest by thinking that you were clearing up the situation.

If people are asking you unusual questions about an event or personal activity, you may be under investigation.

Be aware of your surroundings. When you sense that something unusual is going on, or when people (police or not) start asking you questions about things they would not ordinarily speak to you about, you should assume that you are under investigation. Sometimes officers and detectives use an informant to get close to you and watch your movements, and then report back to the detectives about your relationships and whereabouts.

Interviewer: Is it imperative to consult with an attorney if you suspect that you are under investigation?

Frank: The most common misconception people have about the criminal justice system is that a case will just "go away." That simply does not happen. Detectives will not simply forget about a case.

If you've been in a fight or maybe you were recently stopped for driving under the influence, and the police did not arrest you that night but started investigating you, you should call an attorney immediately. The next logical step is that you will be arrested, so you need an attorney to help protect your rights.

Interviewer: You mentioned police informants? Is that a common practice?

Frank: Yes, and not only in the well-known instance of someone wearing a wire or purchasing items with marked money. Informants can also be utilized in an informal manner. For example, a person was arrested for possession of marijuana and an officer may say, "You can help yourself out here if you work with us."

The person, with no criminal record but who is now facing serious jail time, will do anything to get out of their current predicament. They therefore agree to provide information about other crimes and illegal activities to the police. Suddenly, that young person shows up at your house inquiring about where they can buy narcotics or stolen "hot" items.

The next thing you know, police officers are sitting in your kitchen, waiting to question you with an impending search or arrest warrant. I cannot overemphasize that you need to be aware of *your surroundings*. Pay attention to things that are happening that don't usually occur.

How Should You Proceed if You Have Been Asked to Answer Questions at a Police Station?

Interviewer: What if the police or detectives call someone and say, "We want to talk to you. Come down to the station." Do they have to go, and does that mean they will be arrested? What should they do in that case? What if the officials say, "We want to search your car or house?"

Are you being asked or are you being commanded to come to the police station?

Frank: Here is the key issue: Are you being *asked* or are you being *commanded* to come to the police station? If they are asking you, you have the absolute right under the state and federal constitutions to say, "No, I do not want to go with you. No, I do not want to answer questions and I don't want to talk to you any further. No, you cannot search my home, No, you cannot search my car."

If you are being *asked*, you have the constitutional right to refuse. If officers or detectives are asking permission, they obviously don't have authority. That is the one thing I try to drill into people's minds. You are ***not*** required to go to the police station and answer questions just because they ask you to do so.

Remember, however, that if they are asking, you are definitely the focus of an investigation, and will probably be arrested or questioned at some point. You may also be presented with an official document such as a warrant to search your property or for your arrest. If they are only asking you, however, you are not required to go. On the other hand, if the officers are telling you, "We have a warrant. Come with us," then you have no choice but to go with them. You must comply if the police have a warrant for your arrest.

Interviewer: So even if asked for permission, should they refuse and call an attorney or should they cooperate? What would you recommend?

Frank: If they are asking permission, say no and immediately contact an attorney.

What Does It Mean if You Are Indicted in Pennsylvania?

Interviewer: What does it mean to be indicted? Is that the same as being arrested or something different?

An indictment is primarily how you are charged with a crime at the federal level, not the state level.

Frank: An indictment is a formal document officially putting you on notice that charges have been filed against you by the federal government. An indictment is more of a federal practice. Technically, you can be indicted in Pennsylvania, but the state does not frequently use the indictment process.

The state will prepare a formal document presented at your arraignment.

At the state level, the official process is started

by a criminal complaint, which is an account by a police officer or detective explaining to a magistrate judge that probable cause exists to arrest and charge you with a crime. After a preliminary hearing, the government will file a criminal information sheet, which contains a formal list of charges against you that is presented to you at your formal arraignment. The criminal information also lists the elements of the crimes that the government will need to prove beyond a reasonable doubt at trial.

At the federal level, the prosecutor, on behalf of the government, goes before a grand jury. They present evidence before the grand jury and then come back with a true bill, which is an indictment stating that, "We believe, on this day, that there is enough evidence to go forward and proceed with a trial and prosecution."

If You Are Arrested, Will You Always Be Eligible For Bail in Pennsylvania?

Bail will be set for your release as long as you are not a flight risk or danger to society.

Interviewer: If someone is arrested, when will they have bail set? When will they not? How is the amount of bail determined?

Bail is typically set within 24 to 48 hours of an arrest.

Frank: Bail will be set when two factors are sat-

isfied: 1) the defendant is not a flight risk, and 2) the defendant is not a danger to society. If you have any failure to appear (FTA) in court in your criminal record, then you will have more difficulty obtaining bail.

Keep in mind that the court wants to make sure you are going to appear at all the court hearings. To ensure this will happen, the court looks at past performance as a reliable indicator of your future performance. The court will consider if you have had any prior FTAs, or if your current arrest has violated the conditions of any existing bond in another pending case.

Let's presume that you have a number of instances in the past where you have missed court appearances. The Court will either set a very high bail or deny bail outright. Additionally, if the government can establish that you are a danger to society (having a history of violent crimes, threatening witnesses, or committing dangerous crimes), then the court will probably set a high bond or deny bond altogether.

Bail is usually set at the initial arraignment.

Within 24 to 48 hours of the arrest, the court will conduct an arraignment to notify you of the charges set forth by the police in the criminal complaint and to set the initial bail. If you are dissatisfied with the amount or conditions of the bail, you can petition a higher court to review the bond.

Bail cannot be punitive. The amount or conditions of your bail should not be imposed to serve as punishment for being charged for a particular offense, or as a result of public outcry or media attention. The primary goals of setting bail are to ensure your appearance at all your scheduled hearings and to protect society, if that is deemed necessary.

How Can You Post Your Bond to Be Released from Jail?

Interviewer: When someone's bail is set, are they required to pay the whole amount in cash or can they pay part of it? What are their options?

Frank: There are several types of bail: non-monetary, release on own recognizance (ROR), straight case, or percentage, which is the most common.

If you are released on your own recognizance or given a non-monetary bond, you will not be required to post any money. Essentially, you are being released with a promise to obey any and all conditions of bail and to appear at all court hearings.

Straight cash and percentage bails are the type that require you or someone you know to post cash or collateral in exchange for your release. A bail bond agency usually charges a percentage of the bail to post a bond, commonly ten percent of the total amount of bail set.

There are numerous bail bond agencies in the area that will take care of the process. They consider your assets and your history for appearing for court appearances to determine the percentage that they will require you to pay them to post your bond.

In the alternative form of bail, the court may set a $10,000 bail at ten percent. The percentage is pre-determined and in most cases, the amount to pay in this situation would be $1,000. Therefore, someone pays to a bail bondsman the appropriate amount and the agency will post the bond on your behalf. Each bail bond agency has its own percentage procedure, so it will vary from agency to agency.

If you don't appear for court, the bail bondsman assumes the responsibility of finding you, at which time you may be arrested for violating the terms of your bail bond. There is a popular TV reality show of a bail bondsman who goes off in search of people who violated the terms of their bond, and tried to flee and avoid court proceedings. You do not ever want to violate the terms of your bail bond.

Can Your Defense Attorney Help to Reduce Your Bail?

Interviewer: As someone's attorney, can you go on behalf of a client and try to get the bail amount lowered or rendered unnecessary? Is that a service that you provide?

Frank: Yes, absolutely. For example, someone

might call us and report, "My son is in jail and the bond has been set at $25,000, the preliminary hearing is coming up soon, and we want to get him out." Once we are retained, we can file a motion to have the bail reviewed prior to the hearing, or we can wait to negotiate the bond and charges at the preliminary hearing. If we are retained after the preliminary hearing, we can file a motion to have bail reduced with the trial court.

Your attorney may be able to arrange an OR PR Bond so that no money or property needs to be paid for your release.

We can also work to get the defendant an OR bond, which allows someone to be released on their own recognizance. An OR/PR bond means a defendant is not required to post any money or property in order to be released from jail. The defendant is only required to provide a signature as a promise to appear for future court appearances.

Interviewer: Will the judge impose other re-

lease conditions for certain defendants? Can the judge lower someone's bail, but impose other conditions on them, such as reporting to a probation officer if they live outside the city?

Frank: Yes. Western Pennsylvania is a very visitor-friendly area. We have world-class healthcare systems, outlet malls, casinos, professional football, baseball and hockey teams, along with several internationally-recognized colleges and universities and their respective athletic teams. In addition, we have additional athletic teams and college students 75 miles down the road in Morgantown, West Virginia.

Many people fly to Pittsburgh to attend some of the games, or rent a car at the airport and drive to Morgantown for games, attend concerts in the cultural district, come for healthcare, or live here temporarily for college. Occasionally, those people get into trouble with the law while in Pittsburgh. In such cases, the charges are filed while in Pittsburgh, but the person actually resides in another state or country.

The arraignment judge who sets the bond can impose conditions that the accused remain in the Commonwealth of Pennsylvania unless they seek leave of court. A condition can then be set whereby a person can get out of jail with the promise that they obtain a drug and alcohol evaluation and comply with the court's recommendations.

Conditions may be imposed on an individual who must answer charges in Pennsylvania but resides out-of-state.

A person can be charged by summons when

charging documents are sent to the person's house instead of being formally arrested and carried away in handcuffs. Once that person presents himself (or herself), the defendant is taken to jail pending arraignment and bond.

When people visit Pittsburgh and make bad decisions that lead to criminal charges involving non-violent crimes, the investigating officer may charge the defendant by *summons*, meaning that the officer bypasses taking the defendant to jail immediately following the incident. Instead the officer will obtain the defendant's address, release the defendant, and then mail the citation or complaint to the defendant at his or her home address with a notice to appear for a scheduled hearing.

In other cases not filed by summons, the defendant is arrested and taken to a judge for arraignment. In those cases, the judge will consider the defendant's out-of-state residency when setting the bond.

At that time, the judge is thinking as follows: "This defendant lives in Texas, Virginia, Maine, New York, California or Canada, so what can I do as a judge to ensure that they will come back for their hearings?" Then the judge may reason, "Okay. We'll give you an OR bond but you must call in and report or we can transfer supervision back to your state and you can report to your probation officer or agency there."

What to Avoid if You Have Been Arrested in Pennsylvania

Interviewer: What kind of unintentional mistakes do you see people making that may hurt their case? Once they've been arrested, what can they do that makes things worse?

You will not be able to talk your way out of an arrest.

Frank: The number one thing that astounds me is when defendants try to talk their way out of an arrest or an investigation. Arresting officers and detectives know this and play on a defendant's willingness to talk.

Remember: You have the right to remain silent.

These are trained officers who know the situation you are in and know that you are scared simply by their uniform. The officers see it in your eyes and proceed to take a calming approach by saying, "Just tell me what happened, so we can work this out and you can help yourself."

Sadly, only a small percentage of defendants in this situation are wise enough to exercise their right to remain silent and request an attorney. Most times, the officers try to dissuade the defendant by firmly asking "Why do you need an attorney? Only guilty people need an attorney? Are you telling me you are guilty of something? Do you have something to hide?"

When you provide incriminating evidence, the officers will record what you say into their police report.

Before you know it, the person is telling the police everything. "Well, I did this and that." That person has talked their way into an arrest that probably would not have otherwise happened because the officers did not have any evidence of a crime until the person started freely offering an explanation. Think about it this way: If the police had the information they needed, they would not be asking you what happened.

People believe they are entitled to tell their side of the story, and they also believe that absolute innocence guarantees an acquittal or guarantees they will not be arrested. That simply is not the case. People think, "Oh, I didn't do anything, I don't have anything to hide. It was a clear case of self-defense, so I'll tell you everything." That often ends with people talking themselves into criminal charges and a jail cell.

Television shows are ficticious; your case will not proceed as the cases do on television.

Interviewer: Are there any other mistakes they commonly make?

Frank: Volunteering to speak with police under the mistaken impression that they will talk themselves out of an arrest is the biggest one. That is the one that hurts the most because everything a person says to the officer or detective goes into a report. Usually, a statement is not recorded verbatim in the report. Instead, the officer's understanding and interpretation of what was said goes into the report. Some of it gets lost in the translation, but what they write is going to be cast in a light that makes their case stronger.

Interviewer: What are some of the top misconceptions people have about the criminal process?

Frank: On many occasions, people conclude that if they didn't do anything, there is no way they are going to be found guilty. Or they think, "Oh, this is how it should work because this is how I saw it works on TV.

They don't have my DNA evidence or they don't have all these witnesses, video surveillance, radio or wire taps. The cops don't have any of this information, therefore, it will automatically be an acquittal."

Probably the most common misconception about the criminal process is the misguided belief that "The officer didn't read me my rights for this DUI or public intoxication, so my case should be thrown out."

There are many misconceptions produced by TV shows causing people to think that what transpires in an hour-long show will translate into real life. Trust me, it does not.

Your Miranda Rights and an Arrest

Interviewer: Now that you mention Miranda Rights, how do Miranda Rights come into play, such as the right to remain silent? When do you have them? When do you not?

Frank: When you are the target of an investigation and the officers come to you, pick you up, and take you to the police station, you are the target of an investigation. When you are in custody of officers and not free to leave, that scenario should be construed as the equivalent of an arrest. In this case, the officers are required to advise you of your Miranda Rights prior to an interrogation.

Miranda Rights are only required to be read to you when you are subjected to a custodial interrogation. If you are free to leave, or if the police are not asking you questions, officers are not required to read you the rights.

If you are in custody and cannot leave, the police must read your Miranda Rights to you.

They must read you your Miranda warning because they must tell you of your right to remain silent at this point. Anything you say can and will be used against you in the court of law. You have the right to an attorney. If you can't afford one, one will be appointed to you. Do you understand these rights as I read them to you? Yes. Are you willing to waive these rights and speak to police?

Many times, people think, "Well, they should read those to me at all times." No, they should not. Miranda only comes into play when you are in police custody ***and*** not free to leave ***and*** the officers are about to question you about a crime. The warnings are important because you must be advised of your right against self-incrimination before a police interrogation because that's when you can say something that may hurt you.

Our advice to clients: Refuse to waive your right, refuse to speak, and request an attorney.

People often come to our office and say, "Well, they came in and searched my home but they never read me my rights. Can't you just throw the case out?"

Miranda only applies when officers fail to advise you of your rights, then they question you and you say something that harms you. That is when it becomes an issue because then you were not formally made aware of your rights. Therefore, a defense attorney can challenge the admissibility of your statements in a pre-trial motion before a judge.

Which Is the Right Way to Refuse to Answer Any Police Questions?

Interviewer: I'm sure police pressure people into talking, so how do you refuse without resisting arrest or making your situation worse?

It is important to remain calm and speak politely to the officers.

Frank: I don't want to say that officers pressure people, but I know officers strongly encourage defendants to talk. To assert your right to remain silent, it's all about how you say it. In a perfect world, when you say, "Officer, I wish to speak with an attorney, I don't wish to speak to you right now. I don't wish to answer any questions" and you do so in a calm voice and in control of your emotions, which means you are not screaming or yelling, your request should be honored and the questions should stop. We, however, do not live in a perfect world.

People get into trouble when they begin yelling, become belligerent, and get demanding. It looks and sounds bad, and gives the impression that you are not under control of your emotions and possibly subject to persuasion by additional questioning or prompting.

Self-Representation, Public Defenders or Private Attorneys: Which Option Is Best for You When You Are Facing Criminal Charges?

Interviewer: In terms of representing yourself, what are the pros and cons of getting a public defender, or hiring a private attorney like you?

Public defenders are highly qualified and dedicated attorneys, but typically they carry a large volume of cases.

Frank: Public defenders have a bad reputation in the community. They are typically highly-qualified and dedicated attorneys. There are plenty of private attorneys who owe some of their knowledge and training to the years they spent as public defenders.

This is because public defenders are daily in front of judges and juries, fighting the good fight, and doing what needs to be done to help people in need. It has been suggested that most seasoned public defenders have forgotten more law and procedure than most private attorneys would ever remember or learn.

Public defenders have limited time to devote to each client. Many people prefer the continuity of their relationship with a private attorney.

The downside of public defenders is that they typically carry a high case volume and cannot devote the amount of time to your case that it deserves. Sadly, your perception becomes your reality, especially if you are in jail for the first time and you see a public defender for a short period of time before your hearing. In most cases, regardless of the result of the hearing, you are still upset because you needed or wanted to spend more time.

It is easy to assume that public defenders are brushing you off but in reality, they usually don't need much information from you because they have handled numerous cases similar in nature to your case and have an idea of how it should be resolved. From your perspective, however, you want to meet with them to give them the information you think they should have and advise them as to how your case should be resolved.

A private attorney can devote more time and resources to build a defense.

Often, public defenders get the minimum necessary from you to go forward, which could be acceptable in some cases. In most cases, however, a little bit more time and emphasis needs to be devoted to certain issues like pre-trial motions and investigations. Additionally, sometimes you will get a different public defender at each hearing, which makes continuity difficult to achieve. How can you build any relationship with your public defender? You need to make sure you are both on the same page.

"Self-representation is having a fool for a client." - Anonymous

When you hire a private attorney, you are getting that attorney's attention along with that of their staff. This fosters a healthy attorney-client relationship, and provides you with the consistency you need to feel comfortable when you place your rights and freedoms in the hands of the attorney you have chosen. You know that when you hire a private attorney, you will be able to call that attorney, even during evenings and on weekends, and be able to reach him or her, or at least receive callback promptly. The private attorney should go to the scene, review evidence, conduct further investigation, and uncover additional evidence on your case. Your private attorney should have specialized knowledge of the law as it applies to your particular case.

Private attorneys should review documents with you at a time that is convenient for you, including evenings or weekends. You should be represented by the same attorney in the beginning, middle, and end of your case. There's a certain trust that you should develop with your private attorney that you ordinarily would not be able to build with a public defender.

Interviewer: Is it foolish to defend yourself?

Frank: Absolutely. You are asking to get yourself railroaded. There are few instances where people have successfully defended themselves and have obtained a result that a licensed attorney would have received. The age-old adage is true: *People, including lawyers, who defend themselves have a fool for a client.*

Most laypeople do not understand the impact of pleading guilty to a charge. Any conviction on your criminal record has long-term consequences. Only a trained lawyer can fully explain to you how a guilty plea can impact your record, including guilty pleas to minor traffic offenses.

Any Conviction Has Long-Term Effects

For example, I recently resolved a case where the client had a reckless driving citation. He pled guilty to a traffic citation prior to contacting our office. He said, "Well, I thought I would just pay it and be done with it. It is only a hundred bucks." He paid the citation and then a week later got a letter from the Pennsylvania Department of Transportation, which stated, "You just were found guilty of reckless driving. You're going to lose your driving privileges for six months."

He was surprised because he thought he knew what he was doing. He did not know the collateral effects of pleading guilty and paying this citation. Additionally, because of his guilty plea, he was going to accrue points on his license, and lose that license for a lengthy period of time. Thankfully, we were able to appeal the conviction, and get the conviction overturned without any license suspension or points.

You must consult with an attorney about the options when considering entering a plea.

You should definitely speak with an attorney before you make any decisions on your case. We went to school, obtained the necessary training through years of service, and labored with the books, cases, statutes, and rules to make sure we how to properly represent you and your interests.

Attorneys must prepare for and pass the bar exam in order to be permitted to practice law. On top of the bar exam, there is a great deal of training that we must complete to ensure that we are competent to represent you. Finally, the Pennsylvania Disciplinary Board requires all attorneys to complete hours of continuing education each year. In sum, this is our profession, and we have worked hard to become ready, willing, and able to best represent you.

Therefore, it is important to consult with an attorney before you make any decisions on your case. If you are facing criminal charges of any kind, just pick up the phone and place the call us to make sure that your rights are protected.

Subsequent offenses have enhanced penalties when you have a conviction on your record.

Interviewer: How often is someone who pleads guilty to a low-level charge positioned for more problems if they ever get in trouble again?

Frank: Let's stay with the example I just gave about pleading guilty to reckless driving. In Pennsylvania, we have summary offenses, which are a bit higher than traffic tickets but lower than misdemeanors. People think, "Well, I got a summary offense for public urination, public intoxication, disorderly conduct, or underage drinking. I'll just plead guilty to it. No worries."

After that, you plead guilty, paid the fine, and walked away. You were probably thinking, "I didn't have to pay for a lawyer. I took care of it myself. I'm feeling good about it."

It Is Increasingly Common for Employers to Run Background Checks on Prospective Employees.

Then a year later, you apply for a job and the employer does a background check. Your summary offenses might show up as "public urination," and you are left to explain to your future employer why you were urinating in public. It's a recipe for disaster, and likely will prevent you from getting that job.

You originally thought, "Oh! It's just a fine!" No, it's more than that. It's on your record and you're unable to get it expunged until five years after the conviction, if you do not get into any more trouble. It comes back to haunt you again and again. This may not have happened had you called an attorney first, rather than trying to represent yourself.

Interviewer: Even if it seems like no big deal at the time, you should always consult with an attorney, even for a first offense? Is that what you're saying?

You should always know what your options are after being arrested. Most attorneys offer a free initial consultation.

Frank: Exactly. You should always take every

step to protect your rights, and to make sure that you are doing what is best for you and your case. The essential first step is calling an attorney.

Can You Ever Expect to Receive "Mercy" from the Court?

Interviewer: Let's say you are in the middle of representing a client and they say, "I can't take it anymore. I just want to give up, plead guilty, or I just want to throw myself at the mercy of the court." What do you say to people when that occurs? Is there any such thing as mercy from the court?

Frank: Yes. I try to explain to clients all the possible outcomes, along with when and how they could happen. In addition, I want to explain the worst- and best-case scenario for each situation.

Giving up is one of the worst mistakes you can make after you have been arrested.

A lot of people think, "I'll just plead guilty and get it over with because I want this behind me." That is one of the biggest mistakes you can make. My clients always know up front what is likely to transpire in the courtroom, based upon the prosecutor, the distinct facts of the case, and whether or not the case is being tried in front of a jury or a judge.

Once again, most clients are unaware of the long-reaching effects and how a conviction can impact your future. For example, with sex offenses, a person can think, "I have a minor offense. If I plead guilty, I

can get out of jail today. I've been in jail for six months awaiting trial, and if they offer me a plea for probation, I'm going to take it."

Inevitably, here is what happens: You plead guilty, are required to register as a sex offender under Megan's Law, and then you realize that you are unable to move, work, or do anything without first notifying the State Police. In some instances, your guilty plea will contain a provision prohibiting you from having any contact with your own children without supervision, or from using a computer or the Internet. Further, you find yourself on a public website as a sex offender, and everywhere you move, you will be introduced as John or Jane Doe, the sex offender who lives at the end of the street.

I frequently remind people that they must be wary when they get involved in the criminal justice system. Whatever attorney you retain, you must ask to have everything explained to you, including the possible consequences of pleading guilty.

What Are Reasonable Expectations after You Have a Criminal Charge?

Interviewer: Every case is different, but what's a reasonable expectation somebody can have?

Frank: The most reasonable expectation is to have no expectations until you talk your entire case through with an experienced attorney. By consulting with a qualified attorney, you will learn what the possibilities are, what the possible outcomes may be, and when you can expect to achieve those outcomes.

It is uneasonable to compare your case to someone with another case and expect the same outcome.

It's unreasonable when people say to me, "I want you to guarantee me that this goes away." You will never get that guarantee because such guarantees are not only impossible, they are also unethical.

Some people's expectations are unreasonable. If you are caught on camera committing an offense; there are two or three witnesses who saw what you did; your DNA is found at the scene; you submitted a written confession; you have a track record of committing the crime for which are now suspected of committing, then your suggested guidelines that determine what your sentence should be, will indicate that you should receive no less than five years of prison.

If you think you should get probation simply because someone else in another case got probation for their charges, even though that person was a first-time offender, you are sadly mistaken.

It is unreasonable to compare yourself to someone else because every case is different and unique. Every case contains a distinct set of dynamics, facts, and aggravating and mitigating factors, which will contribute to determine the actual sentence you receive.

An experienced criminal attorney can point out those differences and help manage the expectations of the client.

How an Attorney's Reputation Lends Them Credibility in the Courtroom

Interviewer: How often are you able to make some kind of positive impact on the outcome in a case? For example, have you had an outcome with less jail time or lower fines than was prescribed?

Frank: In most cases, I can negotiate a lower sentence or otherwise have a positive impact on the case. This is because of my extensive and positive history with the prosecutors and police officers. When you have been picking a jury and negotiating with police officers and prosecutors for as many years as I have, you earn a reputation for being prepared and willing to fight for your client. You are known as a person who is knowledgeable of the law, the frequent case-law updates, available defenses, and all possible penalties.

With this background, the prosecutors are more willing to listen to you when you point out the weaknesses in their case, giving you a distinct advantage when negotiating for the best possible result for your client.

I am a strong believer that my clients must be proactive in their criminal case.

After attorneys practice criminal defense law for a number of years, they start to see the same set of facts. They begin to know what to expect and how clients should best prepare themselves to assist in a client's defense. We know to ask: *Does my client need to do community service before the hearing? Does he or she need to anger management classes or a diversionary program like AA or NA meetings prior to appearing in court? Or do they need to get a job or work on obtaining a GED to demonstrate their ability to be a productive citizen and a positive contributor to society?*

Most judges look favorably upon a defendant's proactive actions.

I know that with a certain set of facts, being proactive in your defense causes judges and prosecutors to look favorably upon those efforts. These actions frequently influence the prosecutors and judges to reduce, and often dismiss, the charges against you.

For example, if you are charged with simple assault, DUI, fake ID, public intoxication, or underage drinking as a first-time offender, an experienced attorney should know what proactive steps you can take prior to your preliminary hearing that will aid in the negotiation of your charges.

The Different Levels of Charges in Pennsylvania

Interviewer: What are the different levels of offenses in the Commonwealth of Pennsylvania? You've talked of summary offenses. What about misdemeanors and felonies?

1. Felonies, Misdemeanors and Summary Offenses

Frank: There are three levels of felonies and misdemeanors: first, second, and third degree. First-degree of each category constitutes the highest grading, while third-degree of each is the lowest. Anything below third-degree misdemeanors are summary offenses.

2. Potential Penalties for Felony and Misdemeanor Charges

For a felony of the first degree, the maximum penalty is 20 years in prison and the maximum fine is $25,000. For a felony of the second degree, the maximum penalty is ten years in prison and maximum fine of $25,000. For a felony of third degree, the maximum penalty is seven years in prison and a fine of $15,000. For a misdemeanor one charge, the maximum penalty is five years in prison and a $10,000 fine. For a misdemeanor two, the maximum penalty is two years and a fine of $5,000; and misdemeanor three is subject to one year and a $2,500 fine. Summary offenses are subject to a maximum penalty of 90 days in jail and a $300 fine.

Indictable Offenses in Pennsylvania

Interviewer: What's the process for a misdemeanor versus a felony? Will you explain how these differ from a summary offense?

Frank: Anything graded above a summary offense is what they call an "indictable offense" in Pennsylvania. At the state level, we don't have an official indictment process, but we still say indictable offense because you will go through a formal arraignment process, get a criminal information sheet, and your case will proceed to a judge that sits on the Court of Common Pleas. It is possible that your charges will go past a preliminary hearing to the formal arraignment process and a trial.

When arrested for a felony or misdemeanor such as a robbery, DUI, or burglary, you will most likely be processed, arraigned, and placed in jail before you are able to post bail.

An indictable offense usually involves an arrest and a formal charging process.

For some non-violent offenses, such as shoplifting or theft, you could be notified of your charges through a summons process, which is a set of documents that you receive in the mail. They identify the preliminary charges against you along with the time and location of your preliminary hearing.

A Timeline of Arrest through Resolution

Interviewer: What is the criminal process from the time you are arrested through resolution? What are the different stages called? How long does each take to happen?

1. Arrest, Processing through the Jail, Bail, Preliminary Hearing

Frank: Once arrested, you are processed through the jail, and you will usually have an arraignment within

12 to 48 hours, depending on whether it is a weekend, a weekday, or a holiday. The arraignment is when your initial bond is set and your charges are read to you by the arraignment judge. The date for your preliminary hearing is also set by the arraignment judge and usually scheduled within 7-10 days of your arraignment.

2. Preliminary Hearing and Prima Facia Evidence

At the preliminary hearing, the Commonwealth is required to establish the charges against you by *prima facia* evidence. Only two things need to be proven: 1) that a crime was committed; and 2) that you are likely the person who committed the crime. Aspects of a trial such as credibility, bad acts, character evidence, and the like are not at issue during the preliminary hearing.

3. The Formal Arraignment

If those two things are established at the preliminary hearing, the charges are *held for court,* and the case transferred to the Court of Common Pleas. The next step after the preliminary hearing is the formal arraignment, which is scheduled somewhere between 30 to 45 days after your preliminary hearing.

4. Filing Motions to Dismiss or Suppress Evidence and Obtaining the Criminal Information

The formal arraignment is one of the most important hearings in the criminal process. There you will be provided a copy of the criminal information, which is the formal list of charges against you. Furthermore, your attorney can enter his appearance, request the discovery materials in your case (including police reports), and begin preparing to file any applicable pre-trial motions (such as motions to dismiss, to suppress evidence, or to compel further discovery). Finally, you are assigned to a judge, who will preside over your case for the remainder of the trial process, and assigned a date for your pre-trial conference.

5. The Pre-Trial Conference

The pre-trial conference is when your attorney meets with the prosecutor assigned to your case. The prosecutor will begin to discuss plea negotiations with your attorney and review the suggested sentencing guidelines based upon the crimes charged and your criminal history.

If you are unable to negotiate a resolution for the case at the pre-trial conference, you schedule a date for a plea or a non-jury or jury trial.

6. Trial

If you are incarcerated, your trial must commence within 180 days of the criminal complaint being filed against you. If it is not, you may petition for a nominal bond.

You have a right to a speedy trial.

In all criminal cases at the state level, you are entitled to a speedy trial, which means that you are entitled to have your trial commence within 365 days of the date of the filing of a criminal complaint against you, excluding any delays caused by the defense. If your trial does not begin within that time period, your defense attorney could petition the court for a dismissal pursuant to the Rules of Criminal Procedure.

After the pre-trial conference, a trial date is scheduled depending on the schedules of the court, prosecutor, and defense attorney. The trial could be scheduled as early as a few of weeks or few months, depending on the timing calculated for the speedy trial rule.

If you are found guilty after a trial, sentencing must be scheduled within 90 days. After sentencing, your appellate rights are triggered and you have ten days to file post-sentence motions, which may include challenges to the weight and sufficiency of the evidence presented at trial or a challenge to the discretionary aspects of your sentence.

Sentencing is 90 days after trial; post-sentence motions must be filed within 10 days after sentencing.

If you plead guilty, you have ten days after sentencing to file a post-sentence motion to withdraw that plea. Whether after trial or after a plea, the trial judge must rule on the motions within 120-150 days.

If the judge denies the motions, you have 30 days to file a notice of appeal to the Superior Court.

If the trial judge does not rule on your post-sentence notions within the allotted time, the motions will be deemed denied by operation of law. Once the motions are denied, you have 30 days to file a direct appeal by filing a notice of appeal to Superior Court, which is the intermediate appellate court in Pennsylvania.

Once you file your notice of appeal with the Superior Court, you will then file a brief with the court and present oral arguments, if you so choose. By law, your appeal to the Superior Court is an appeal of right, which means that you are entitled to counsel and to have your appeal heard by the Superior Court.

If the Superior Court denies the appeal, you may petition the Supreme Court for Allowance of Appeal.

Should the Superior Court deny your appeal, you may petition the Pennsylvania Supreme Court for allowance of appeal. You do not have a right to this appeal. The Supreme Court chooses whether to accept your case or not. If the Pennsylvania Supreme Court declines to review your appeal, your sentence becomes final in state court 90 days after you receive the notice of denial from the Pennsylvania Supreme Court.

Once your sentence becomes final, you have one year from that day to file a PCRA petition, in which you may argue that your attorney was ineffective or point out any other Constitutional defects that occurred during your trial or appeal.

If You Go To Trial, the Process Can Take More Than a Year to Resolve

Interviewer: How long does the process take, in general?

Frank: If you were going to trial, starting from the time you were arrested, a trial date could be scheduled anywhere from eight to ten months after that. In my experience, that's about average.

Postponements for a variety of reasons, however, are common, and are requested by the Commonwealth and defense alike. When you factor in those postponements, often your case is not resolved at the trial level for up to one year after you were initially arrested.

A small percentage of criminal cases go to trial. Most are resolved in plea bargains.

Interviewer: What percentages of your cases go to trial as opposed to being resolved in a plea agreement?

Frank: I would say that 70 to 80 percent plead out, if not more. Very few of cases go to trial.

How Long Can It Take to Reach a Plea Agreement with the Prosecutor?

Interviewer: If you end up agreeing to a plea agreement, how long can it take on average?

Frank: It depends. Sometimes it takes just as long to negotiate a favorable plea bargain as it does to get to trial. In those cases, you are looking at approximately one year from the date you are arrested. When it is clear you are not interested in contesting the charges, however, there are various programs that may expedite the process for you, such as EDP or ARD.

1. Opting for an EDP or ARD

EDP is short for Expedited Disposition Plea. At

the preliminary hearing, depending on the facts of your case, the prosecutor may present you with an EDP offer. You also may be eligible for a program called ARD, which is short for Accelerated Rehabilitative Disputation. The ARD program is mostly for first time non-violent offenders, for such things as DUIs or theft cases where the amount of restitution is under $10,000. Once you successfully complete the ARD program and pay fines and court costs, your case can be expunged from your record as if it never occurred.

An experienced criminal defense attorney can usually surmise by the allegations in the criminal complaint and by taking a quick look at your criminal history whether you would be eligible for the EDP or ARD program. If eligible, you could have your case resolved relatively quickly, usually within four to six months.

2. Phoenix Court Plea

You may also be eligible for the Phoenix Court Program, which is reserved for non-violent offenders who are not eligible for the ARD program. Usually the Phoenix Court Program is for second-time DUI Offenders and other non-violent offenders with a criminal history that renders them ineligible for the ARD program.

Diversionary courts expedite the process in plea bargains

When May You Be Offered a Diversion Program or Alternate Punishment?

Interviewer: This leads into the diversion programs and alternative punishments. What other kinds of diversions or alternative punishments are there for certain offenses?

Frank: That depends to which program you are being admitted. For instance, EDP offers are made at the preliminary hearing. Let's say you go to the preliminary hearing for a first-time, drug-trafficking offense but you are really a drug abuser as opposed to a drug trafficker. Since you were buying in bulk, so to speak, it appears to prosecutors and investigators that you are a drug trafficker because of the quantity of drugs you purchased.

An experienced defense attorney will negotiate with the prosecutor and arresting officers to highlight the differences and the case-specific facts that indicate you are a drug user. If successful, the attorney can negotiate a plea agreement allowing you to plead guilty to simple possession of the drugs, a misdemeanor, as opposed to possession of those drugs with the intent to deliver them, which is a felony. You would be able to take this plea in front of a trial judge at the preliminary hearing in the form of an EDP plea.

The defense attorney could also negotiate a guilty plea through the Phoenix Court Program by setting the wheels in motion at the preliminary hearing. Let's say you are facing a first-time DUI charge and because you already have a guilty plea on your record for retail theft within the last ten years, you are ineligible for the ARD program. An experienced attorney can negotiate with the prosecutor to have your case considered for the Phoenix Court Program while the case is still at the preliminary hearing.

If agreeable, the prosecutor will mark the file for consideration of the Phoenix Court Program, you will then receive verification of acceptance into the program at the formal arraignment and scheduled for a plea date even before your pre-trial conference. In this instance, your case could be resolved relatively quickly after your preliminary hearing.

Interviewer: Are there any other diversion programs or alternative punishments?

1. DUI Court for Third-Time DUI Offenders

Frank: Yes, there is DUI Court for third-time DUI offenders. Entry into this can usually be negotiated at the pre-trial conference. If accepted, you enter into the DUI Court program and to successfully complete the program, you will be subject to random urine screening, safety classes, and a probationary period. You will be required to meet with a probation officer and participate in review hearings with the judge in charge of the DUI program. This program is in lieu of the mandatory one year in prison that normally comes with third time DUIs.

2. Drug Court

Drug Court is a program for repeat drug offenders who have been identified as drug users as opposed to drug traffickers. The creators of Drug Court recognized the need to address drug abuse, the driving force behind many of the crimes committed. Through Drug Court, more attention is devoted to addiction. The focus is on treatment and rehabilitation, as opposed to punishment.

3. Veterans' Court

Veterans' Court is for individuals who are dealing with the difficulties of being military veterans who commit crimes primarily as a result of Post-Traumatic Stress Disorder. In Veterans' Court, defendants are exposed to specialized treatment and rehabilitation with experienced counselors and social workers throughout a strict probationary period coupled with court review hearings.

4. Mental Health Court

Mental Health Court is primarily for offenders who have been diagnosed with mental health issues identified as the cause for one to repeatedly-committed crimes. Once again, the focus is treatment, not punishment, during a probationary period and strict review hearings with the supervising trial judge.

Attorney Walker Handles All Levels of Criminal Offenses in His Practice

Interviewer: What are the most common crimes for which you end up representing people?

Frank: Every time I think I've seen it all, someone comes in with a different set of facts. For the most part, I've represented people charged with everything from traffic offenses to first-degree murder. I've handled the heavy-hitter drug case, bank robberies, high-level conspiracies, sex offenses, shoplifting, and even appeals to the State Superior and Supreme Court. Additionally, I have taken cases before the United States Court of Appeals and the United States Supreme Court.

I frequently receive calls from clients charged with a variety of offenses such as DUI and people charged with summary offenses like under-age drinking, fake ID, public intoxication, disorderly conduct, or

public urination. I like to call the summary offenses "paper cut crimes" because people often think summary offenses are small and unimportant, just like a paper cut. In reality, a conviction for a summary offense can really hurt you if left untreated.

The most common example is the summary offense for having a fake ID. Let's say you are a college student, go to a bar, and use a fake ID. You get arrested, plead guilty, and the next thing you know, your driver's license is suspended.

I also receive numerous calls for more serious cases such as homicide, including murder and manslaughter, sex offenses, white collar crimes, federal indictments and violent crimes. Additionally, I am one of the few attorneys in the area qualified to accept and handle death penalty cases.

Although most calls are from clients or family members on behalf of clients, on many occasions I receive calls and referrals from other attorneys in other areas of law or from law firms that do not have the experience to handle serious criminal matters.

Interviewer: What have you learned about people's behavior, their reactions to being arrested, and then going through the criminal justice system? What insights did you gain about the human side of the process?

Frank: People genuinely want concrete answers and guidance. Infrequent participants in the criminal justice system want someone to guide them through the process and explain what happened, what is going to happen, when it will happen, and what the final result will be.

The most common questions I receive are: Am I

going to jail? Am I going to have to pay all these fines? How is this criminal case going to impact my life in the long run? Will I be able to work with these charges? Will I be able to keep my kids if I'm found guilty? The main thing I've noticed is that people want answers.

Will Your Criminal Charge Become Public Knowledge?

Interviewer: When someone is accused of a crime, how public is their situation going to be? Will their family and friends find out?

Pennsylvania does have public access to criminal charges.

Frank: We have a public docket in Pennsylvania where you can look up a case with nothing more than the correct spelling of a person's first and last name. You can look up the case and view the list of charges and upcoming court dates. However, the public system does not permit access to the specific allegations set forth in the criminal complaint or the discovery.

Occasionally, your case may garner the attention of the local news. Those news outlets may send a camera to some of your court proceedings in an attempt to obtain a statement or video footage of you walking from the courthouse. If so, the footage will be on television and the public will know about your case.

Ordinarily, most cases do not garner media attention. Unless someone has a reason to research your name on the public docket, they will not learn about your DUI, theft offense, simple assault, or other criminal offenses.

What Can You Do to Minimize Your Anxiety During the Process of Resolving a Criminal Charge?

Interviewer: How have you seen people best keep their head together while they're going through this process so their whole world doesn't fall apart?

Frank: I tell it to them straight. Clients want certainty, but there are no absolutes in the law. I inform my clients as to what they should reasonably expect throughout the course of the proceeding, including all the possible variables, but without any guarantees. When you demonstrate the ability to answer the questions based on your experience, clients tend to listen.

To get the best results in a case, I often tell a client that it is in their best interest to perform some action, such as community service or a drug and alcohol evaluation, before their hearing. What's more, I advise clients not to have any contact with certain people, to

stay out of social media, to get a job, or to go back to school. In the meantime, I warn them to keep their head down, stay out of trouble, and spend time with their family.

If they do what I tell them to do, then I will handle the rest. Once you hire me, your problems officially become my problems. I don't need you worrying about the case, I need you to be calm. I need you to worry about what you *can* control because you can't control what has already happened. Nothing you do can change the facts of the crime that has been committed. You are not going to fix the problem, because as your attorney, it is my job to put my effort and experience into resolving the case in your best interest.

Clients tend to listen to me, and when they do, they are able to keep their cool throughout the process. They know that they have someone who has the real-life experience, who's been there, and who has obtained the various positive outcomes time and time again.

I practice in the magistrate, state, and federal courts in Western Pennsylvania and northern West Virginia.

Interviewer: In which courts can you practice? What are the names of the courts that commonly hear your cases?

Frank: I am licensed to practice in Pennsylvania, West Virginia, and the federal courts in Western Pennsylvania and West Virginia. I practice frequently at each level of these courts, from the magistrate courts all the way up to the highest appellate courts.

Interviewer: Do you feel like you know most

of the judges and prosecutors pretty well? Is there a mutual respect that your clients will benefit from because those judges know you?

My good reputation helps to foster mutual respect among the judges and prosecutors. I frequently work with police, which can be beneficial for my clients.

Frank: I think so. I work hard and try to afford people the same respect that I would like to receive in return when I am in the courtroom. This is a profession and should not be taken personally. It all boils down to the fact that prosecutors are doing their job, just like I am doing mine. It doesn't bode well if both of us walk away angry because we disagree on a particular case. The legal community is a tight-knit group and odds are we will meet the same attorney on another matter in the future.

As professionals in the legal field, we can do good things from both sides of the courtroom. I understand that the prosecutors have a way of looking at a case that may be different than how I view the case. These differences are inevitable because I represent an individual's interests, while the Commonwealth represents the interests of the government and its victims. These interests squarely are at odds with each other. Nonetheless, my job is and always will be to be a zealous advocate for my clients. Nothing else will ever trump this priority in my mind.

When I cross-examine a witness or cross-examine a law enforcement professional, I am doing my job, and I want to be prepared to carry out that task to the best of my capabilities. Nonetheless, I try to develop relationships beyond the case because I know that the prosecutors and detectives are going to keep progressing in their career. The attorneys will not be assistant prosecutors forever; some will be move on to become judges, clerks, executives, or defense attorneys. I try to maintain a high level of respect and decorum in each case because my reputation will eventually start to precede me on future cases, in positive and negative ways.

What Should You Look Out For and What Should You Look For When Hiring an Attorney?

Interviewer: What are some of the qualities people should look for when they're interviewing attorneys? What are the positive and negative signs that potential clients should be looking for?

I recommend looking for experience in the area of defense that you need.

Frank: Most people should look around and find an attorney who is experienced in the relevant area of the law. If your son or daughter is facing a homicide charge and an attorney touts on their website and social media that they have extensive experience handling DUI and traffic offenses, you may want to keep looking for another attorney. That DUI attorney may handle DUI cases very well. You may like and even know that DUI attorney. In fact, someone may have referred you to that DUI attorney. Do you really want that DUI attorney handling the homicide trial of your son or daughter with only having experience in DUI cases? No, you do not.

Also, do not just focus on what that attorney is saying about himself (or herself). Focus on what other people are saying about that person. Look at what past clients have said about the attorney. Look at some of the media clips and news articles that may mention the attorney. Search for case results, client testimonies, or published articles.

When meeting with an attorney, he or she should talk about your case and not about themselves.

Call the office and speak with the attorney. How does the attorney present herself? Does the attorney only talk about himself? Does the attorney talk about your case? Most importantly, does the attorney only tell you good things? If the attorney only tells you good things about your case and how it can be resolved, that is a bad sign. An attorney should tell you what is realistic. They should tell you the truth about your case and most often, that truth is not exclusively good news. You should hear something like, "Look, you messed up. This is what you can and can't do. If you're found guilty, this is going to happen. If you're found not guilty, you'll be happy. But here are the most likely outcomes with this set of facts."

If the attorney is able to guide you through the entire process and let you know exactly what to expect, that is an attorney you should consider. You want someone who has been there before, and who is dedicated to fighting for you.

You don't need an attorney who is going to say,

"Oh, I'll do this and I'll do this. I promise you this and I promise you that." The next thing you know, they pass it off to a paralegal and you never speak to that attorney again until your court date. You also do not want an attorney who is going to pass your problems off to one of their associates or refer it to someone else.

Look for an attorney who will be with you every step of the way.

You want to make sure you are dealing with the attorney with whom you consulted and then hired. You not only have an investment in the attorney, but you also have an investment in your future.

I offer the benefit of my experience to my clients. I have learned from both my victories and defeats.

Interviewer: Is there anything else that you would like to tell us about yourself that is of special value to potential clients?

Frank: My main strength is this: *I've been there.* I have won cases and I have lost some cases. The most important thing is that I have learned from each experience along the way. I have also learned from some of the best attorneys and judges out there. We have a great legal system in general, but this is especially true in Western Pennsylvania because of the tight-knit community. I've been fortunate enough to cultivate relationships with some of the finest legal practitioners in the area, and I have learned from each of those relationships.

I know what works and what doesn't work. I am experienced with jury trials, non-jury trials, and hearings. I have obtained not-guilty verdicts and gotten clients out of bad situations time and time again.

I welcome clients to contact my office for a free consultation.

I encourage people to do their research, visit our website, and call the office to schedule a consultation. We're happy to speak with you and go over your information. Our website contains quite a bit of useful information that covers the different crimes, various grading of offenses, and maximum penalties and fines.

Visitors to the website can submit the details of a particular case to me via email. My staff and I will review the information and determine the best course of action to get positive results for you.

My website is **www.FrankWalkerLaw.com.** My nationwide toll-free number is 1-800-496-4143. For local callers, you can call (412) 532-6805 or email questions to: frank@frankwalkerlaw.com.

Frank Walker Law

428 Forbes Avenue, Ste. 1800
Pittsburgh, PA 15219

(412) 532-6805

www.FrankWalkerLaw.com

This publication is intended for informational purposes only. No legal advice is being given and no attorney-client relationship is intended to be created by reading this material. If you are facing legal issues, whether criminal or civil, seek professional legal counsel to get your questions answered.

Made in United States
Troutdale, OR
11/03/2026

56844889R00036